A LOOK AT US HISTORY

THE DECLARATION OF INDEPENDENCE

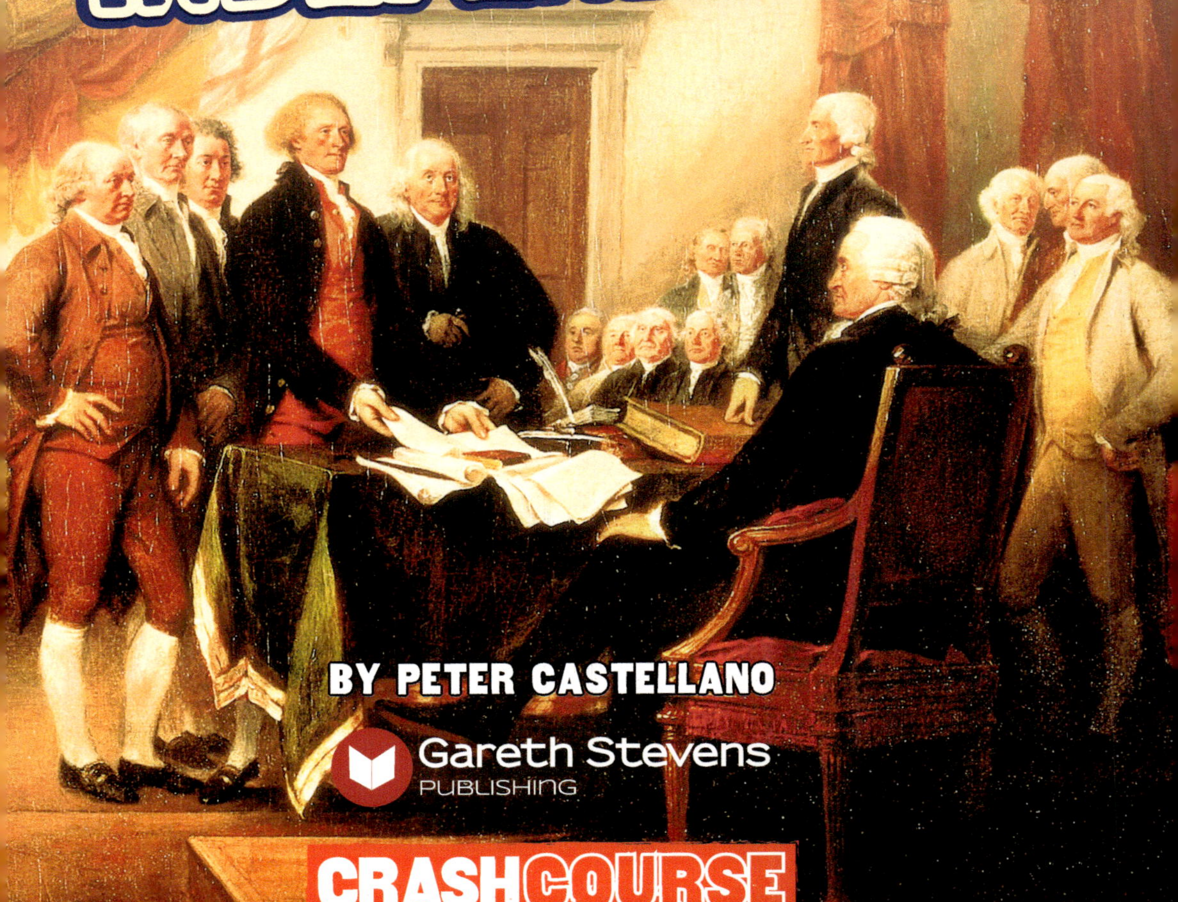

BY PETER CASTELLANO

Gareth Stevens PUBLISHING

CRASHCOURSE

Please visit our website, www.garethstevens.com. For a free color catalog of all our high-quality books, call toll free 1-800-542-2595 or fax 1-877-542-2596.

Cataloging-in-Publication Data
Names: Castellano, Peter.
Title: The Declaration of Independence / Peter Castellano.
Description: New York : Gareth Stevens Publishing, 2018. | Series: A look at US history | Includes index.
Identifiers: ISBN 9781482460315 (pbk.) | ISBN 9781482460339 (library bound) | ISBN 9781482460322 (6 pack)
Subjects: LCSH: United States. Declaration of Independence--Juvenile literature. | United States--Politics and government--1775-1783--Juvenile literature.
Classification: LCC KF4506.C27 2018 | DDC 973.3'13--dc23

First Edition

Published in 2018 by
Gareth Stevens Publishing
111 East 14th Street, Suite 349
New York, NY 10003

Designer: Samantha DeMartin
Editor: Kristen Nelson

Photo credits: Series art Christophe BOISSON/Shutterstock.com; (feather quill) Galushko Sergey/Shutterstock.com; (parchment) mollicart-design/Shutterstock.com; cover, p. 1 DEA PICTURE LIBRARY/De Agostini/Getty Images; p. 5 Matanya/Wikimedia Commons; p. 7 Daderot/Wikimedia Commons; p. 9 traveler1116/Getty Images; p. 11 Stock Montage/Archive Photos/Getty Images; p. 13 Hulton Archive/Archive Photos/Getty Images; p. 15 SuperStock/Getty Images; p. 17 Susan Law Cain/Shutterstock.com; p. 19 Fæ/Wikimedia Commons; p. 21 Three Lions/Hulton Archive/Getty Images; p. 23 UniversalImagesGroup/Universal Images Group/Getty Images; p. 25 Archive Photos/Archive Photos/Getty Images; p. 27 Jean Victor Schnetz/Getty Images; p. 29 Bettmann/Bettmann/Getty Images.

Printed in the United States of America

CPSIA compliance information: Batch #CS17GS: For further information contact Gareth Stevens, New York, New York at 1-800-542-2595.

CONTENTS

Words in the glossary appear in **bold** type the first time they are used in the text.

PROBLEMS WITH THE KING

By the 1770s, the 13 American **colonies** were unhappy with British rule. **Representatives** from 12 colonies met in September 1774 to talk about their problems. They sent the British king a list of **grievances** in October, giving him a chance to address them.

the First Continental Congress

MAKE THE GRADE

The meeting of the 12 colonies in 1774 is called the First Continental Congress.

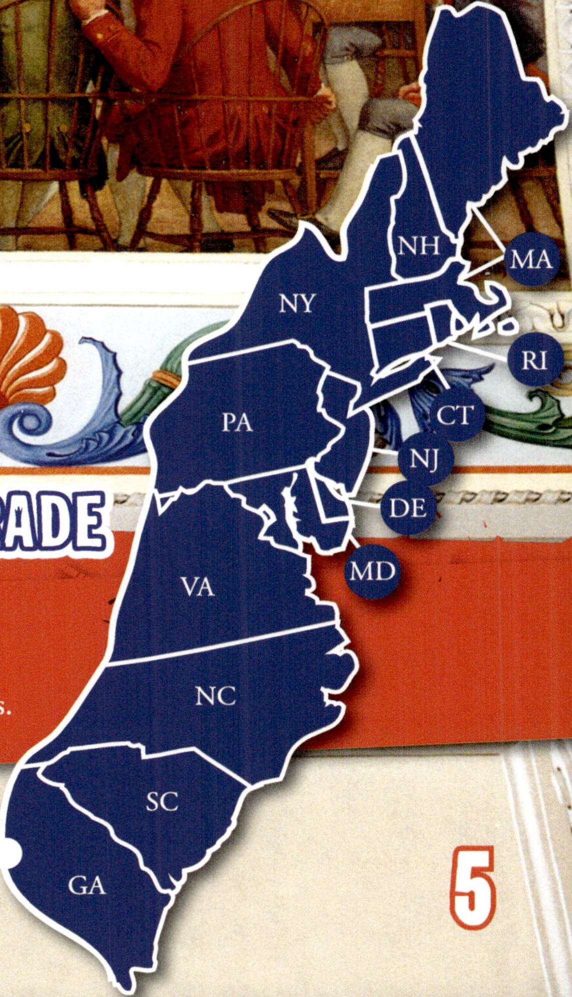

original thirteen colonies

THE CONGRESS

The king never answered. In April 1775, the Battles of Lexington and Concord were fought, beginning the American Revolution. The Second Continental Congress met in May 1775. The representatives were still trying to claim their rights as part of England.

MAKE THE GRADE

The congress acted as the colonies' government during the American Revolution. It raised the Continental army, made money, and even created a post office.

As fighting continued, many colonies believed independence was the only way to gain the rights they wanted. On June 7, 1776, Richard Henry Lee of Virginia presented a **resolution** to the congress. It said the colonies "ought to be, free and independent States."

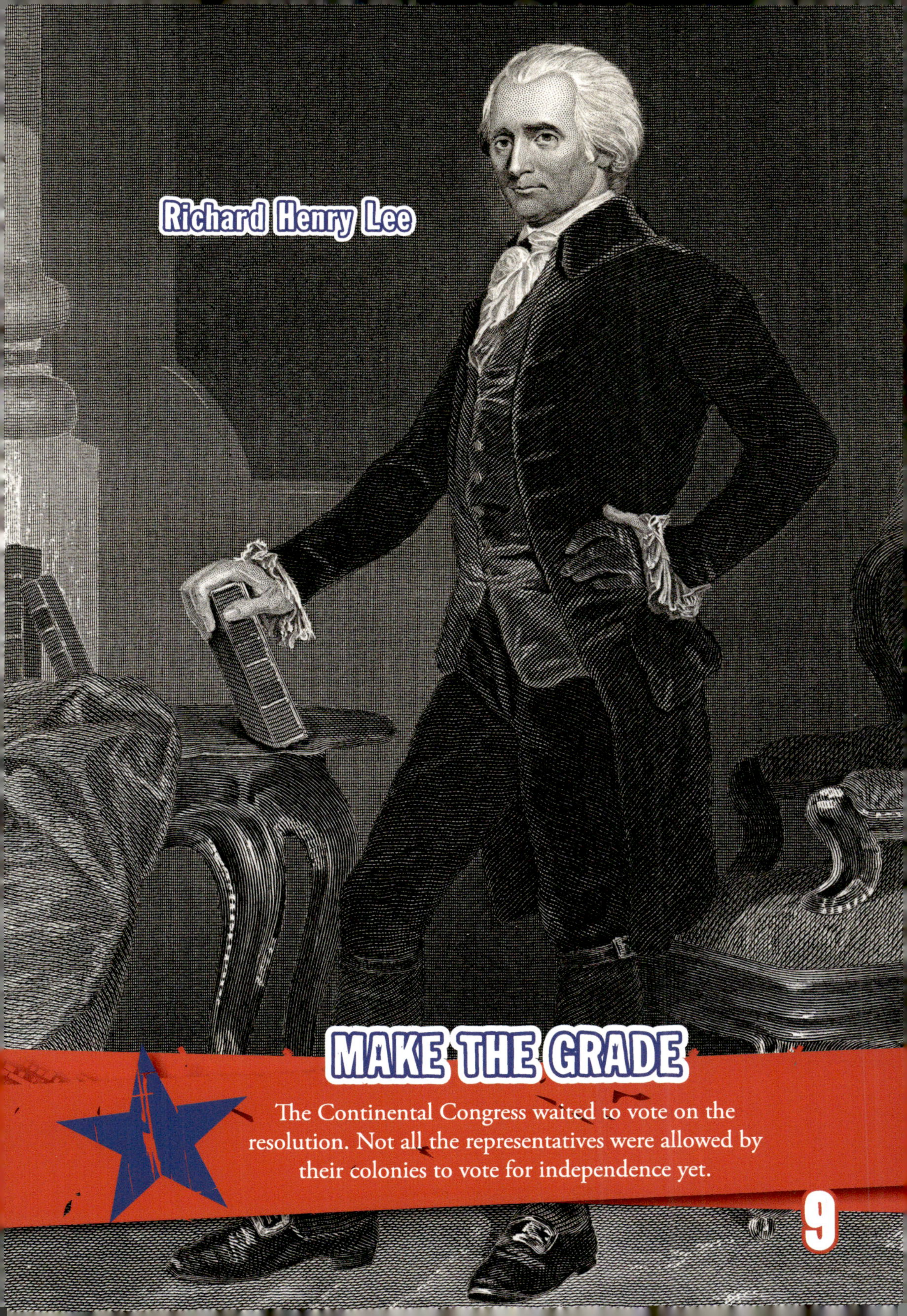

MAKE THE GRADE

The Continental Congress waited to vote on the resolution. Not all the representatives were allowed by their colonies to vote for independence yet.

COMMITTEE OF FIVE

The congress took a 3-week break. During this time, a committee, or group, of five men was chosen to write out why the colonies should be independent. John Adams, Benjamin Franklin, Thomas Jefferson, Roger Sherman, and Robert R. Livingston made up the committee.

MAKE THE GRADE

The committee represented major areas of the colonies, with two men from New England (Adams and Sherman), two men from the middle colonies (Franklin and Livingston), and a southerner (Jefferson).

Jefferson was known as a talented writer and was chosen to do the main writing of the **declaration**. When he was finished, Jefferson asked Adams and Franklin to look at a **draft** of it before they presented it to the congress.

Thomas Jefferson

MAKE THE GRADE

Jefferson was **influenced** by the great thinker John Locke and by George Mason, who wrote Virginia's Declaration of Rights. Thomas Paine's *Common Sense* also influenced Jefferson.

VOTES FOR INDEPENDENCE!

On July 2, 1776, the Lee Resolution for independence passed. Over the next few days, the congress made some changes to the written declaration. A part Jefferson wrote against slavery was cut from the final **document**.

MAKE THE GRADE

The southern states and some New England states wouldn't vote for the declaration if it opposed, or went against, slavery.

WHAT IT SAYS

The beginning of the declaration says the document explains why the colonists want independence. The next main part, the preamble, lists the beliefs people of the time considered true. It says all men have natural rights, including "life, liberty, and the **pursuit** of happiness."

MAKE THE GRADE

The Declaration of Independence simply stated the ideas and wishes of the colonies for their future. It didn't make laws or give anyone rights.

The preamble goes on to say people have a right to overthrow their government if it doesn't serve them. Then they should form a new government of their choosing. It ends by listing the grievances against the British king.

MAKE THE GRADE

Some of the grievances included the king keeping needed laws from being passed and stopping the colonies from forming their own representative bodies.

The declaration then says that the colonies had made their grievances known to the king, but nothing was done. So, having written out the problems for the world to see, they wanted to cut ties with the British crown. Finally, the colonies declare themselves "free and independent states."

MAKE THE GRADE

One reason the colonies wanted to declare independence was to make the French believe in their cause and help them in the war.

APPROVAL

Twelve colonies approved, or agreed to, the Declaration of Independence on July 4. Then, it was taken to a local printer. The first public reading was July 8 in Philadelphia, Pennsylvania. By July 9, all 13 colonies had approved it.

MAKE THE GRADE

Today, the original Declaration of Independence is kept at the National Archives Building in Washington, DC.

The Declaration of Independence was ready to be signed on August 2. John Hancock, the president of the Second Continental Congress, was the first to the sign it. In total, 56 representatives signed the declaration, but some signed after August 2.

MAKE THE GRADE

The signers of the declaration committed treason because the colonies still belonged to the British Empire. Treason is doing something against your country's government with the plan of overthrowing it.

EFFECTS

The Declaration of Independence was signed at the beginning of the American Revolution. It **inspired** the Continental army to keep fighting! But the document was important to others, too. It inspired those working against the French government during the French Revolution soon after!

MAKE THE GRADE

The declaration also influenced a group working to overthrow the Spanish empire in South America.

The Declaration of Independence had an effect long after the colonies became one nation in 1781. President Lincoln **quoted** it in his famous Civil War speech, the Gettysburg Address. Martin Luther King Jr. did, too, during his "I Have a Dream" speech.

MAKE THE GRADE

In 1848, the Declaration of Sentiments, a document stating women's rights, was modeled after the Declaration of Independence.

"...all men, yes black men as well as white men, would be guaranteed the unalienable rights of life, liberty, and the pursuit of happiness."
Martin Luther King Jr., 1963

TIMELINE OF THE DECLARATION OF INDEPENDENCE

June 7, 1776
The Lee Resolution is introduced.

June 11, 1776
Five men are chosen to draft a declaration of colonial independence. The Continental Congress takes a break.

July 1, 1776
The Continental Congress meets again.

July 2, 1776
The Lee Resolution passes. A draft of the Declaration of Independence is introduced.

July 4, 1776
The declaration is approved.

August 2, 1776
Many members of the Continental Congress sign the declaration.